This book belongs to

_____

ISBN-13: 978-0-8249-5570-0

Published by Ideals Children's Books
An imprint of Ideals Publications
A Guideposts Company
Nashville, Tennessee
www.idealsbooks.com

Color separations by Precision Color Graphics, Franklin, Wisconsin
Printed and bound in the United States of America

Library of Congress Cataloging-in-Publication Data
My first book of prayers : poems / selected by Elizabeth Bonner Kea ;
illustrated by Stephanie McFetridge Britt.
      p. cm.
              (alk. paper)
    1. Prayer—Juvenile literature. [1. Prayers.] I. Kea, Elizabeth Bonner,
1976– II. Britt, Stephanie, ill.

BV212 .M9 2000
242'.62—dc21   00-049412

Poems selected by Elizabeth Bonner Kea

Worz_Dec11_2

For Sarah

My First Book of Prayers

Illustrated by

Stephanie McFetridge Britt

ideals children's books

Nashville, Tennessee

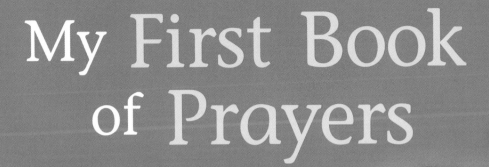

Lord, teach a little child to pray,
And, oh, accept my prayer;
I know you hear the words I say,
For you are everywhere.

Author Unknown

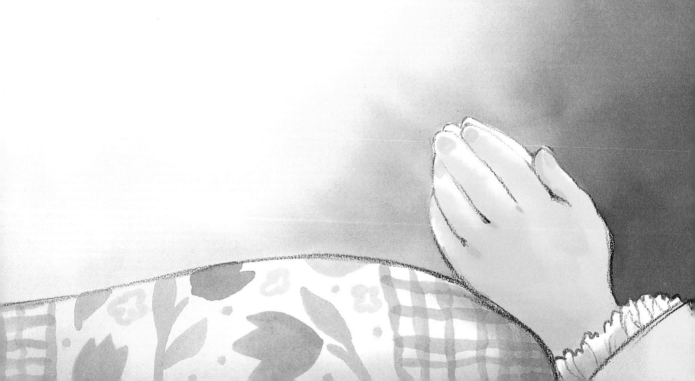

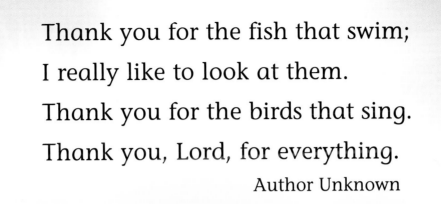

Thank you for the fish that swim;
I really like to look at them.
Thank you for the birds that sing.
Thank you, Lord, for everything.

Author Unknown

For flowers that bloom about our feet,
For tender grass, so fresh and sweet,
For song of bird and hum of bee,
Father in heaven, we thank thee!

For blue of stream, for blue of sky,

For pleasant shade of branches high,

For beauty of the blowing trees,

Father in heaven, we thank thee!

For mother love
    and father care,
For brothers strong
    and sisters fair,
Father in heaven,
    we thank thee!
Ralph Waldo Emerson

For each new morning and its light,

For rest and shelter of the night,

For every gift your goodness sends,

We thank you, loving God.

Author Unknown

Heavenly Father, hear my prayer;

Keep me in thy loving care.

Guide me through each lovely day,

In my work and in my play.

Keep me pure and sweet and true

In everything I say and do.

Abbie Burr

We thank you, Lord,
For birds and flowers,
For trees and winds,
And gentle showers.

We thank you for
Our clothes and food,
For friends and parents,
Kind and good.

Herbert Stoneley

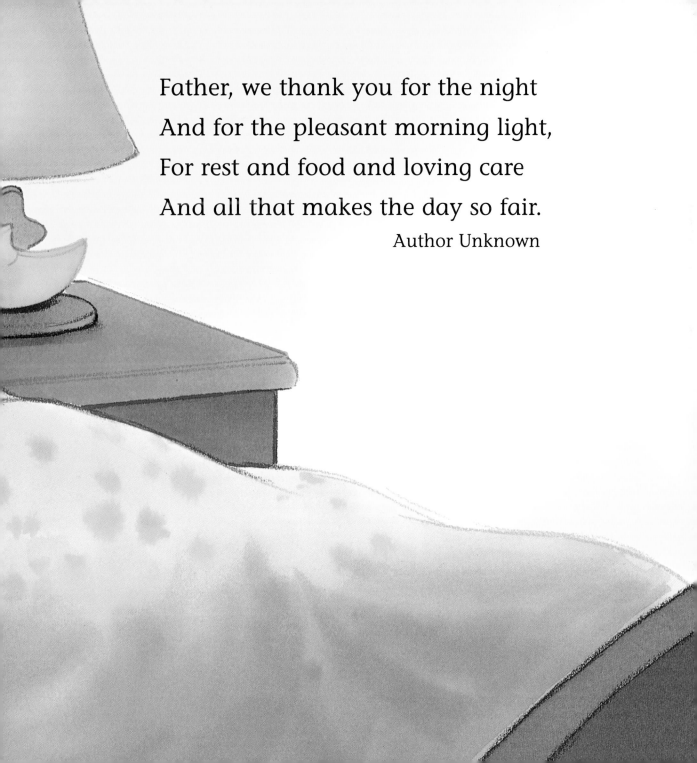

Father, we thank you for the night

And for the pleasant morning light,

For rest and food and loving care

And all that makes the day so fair.

Author Unknown

I see the moon,
And the moon sees me.
God bless the moon,
And God bless me.

Author Unknown

Now I lay me down to sleep;

I pray the Lord my soul to keep.

Watch over me throughout the night

And bring me safe to morning light.

Author Unknown